The Outerspace of God's Love

RICKY CLEMONS

PUBLISHED BY FIEDLI PUBLISHING, INC.

Copyright ©2021, Ricky Clemons

ALL RIGHTS RESERVED.

No part of this publication may be reproduced, stored in a retrieval system, or transmitted in any form or by any means—electronic, mechanical, photo-copy, recording, or any other—except for brief quotation in reviews, without the prior permission of the author or publisher.

ISBN: 978-1-60414-904-3

Published by

Fideli Publishing, Inc.
119 W. Morgan St.
Martinsville, IN 46151
www.FideliPublishing.com

Table of Contents

The Outer Space of God's Love 1

Let's Imagine 3

One Day There Will Be No Righteous Person On Earth 5

We Need to Take Jesus Christ Seriously 7

Jesus Can Use Ordinary People 9

The Years of Our Lives 11

The Truth 13

Throughout the Day and Throughout the Night 15

Love is a Small Word 17

Jesus Was There 19

If You and I Don't Feel Good About 21

The Beautiful Country 23

Laws 25

Old Sinful Ways 27

Is Worthy to be Worshipped 29

You Will Never Regret It 31

Is No Competition Thing 33

Faith in an Unseen God 35

Without You, my Lord Jesus 37

When Jesus Lived on Earth 39

How We are Raised Up 42

Love is Every Good Thing 44

Human Reasoning 45

To Accept 47

You Can Put Your Belief in Jesus Christ 49

It's Good to Love Everyone 51

A New Day May Be 53

Have Sense Enough to Know 55

Death Doesn't Care About 57

Man Can't Tame the Tongue 59

Don't Look at Other People... 61

Convicted 62

You Shouldn't Let It Go to Your Head 64

Uncomfortable 67

If Being Black is a Crime 69

Believe 73

Don't Put Off 74

A Loan from God 75

There is No Retirement in Jesus Christ 77

In God We Trust 78

Jesus Always Cares 79

Jesus Has His 80

The Partly Cloudy Days in Our Lives 81

You Know What it Will Take 82

There are People Who Believe 83

Will Obey Jesus.. 84

Failures	85
The Right Thing to Do	86
Super Intelligent	87
But I Love	88
Up to This Day	89
Look in the Mirror of Self	90
In the Bag of Life	91
Many People Realize	92
Unbelievers Will Not Be Attracted to Our Faith	93
We Can say and Do	94
Mental Health and Physical	95
The Government	96
My Mother's Prayers	97
Is known	98
We Love Life	99
It's Helping Me	100
You Are So Realistic All the Time	101
The Early Morning Light	102
Some Things Do Come Up	103
Life is Always Up to Something	104
There are a Lot of Good People	105
No Matter What We Do for the Lord	106
We Can Tell Jesus	107
Is Eternal	108

Under the Sky 109

In the Mirror of Life 110

One Day I Want to See Jesus Christ 111

Won't Make Any Time for You 112

Some Things We Do Wrong 113

Especially in the Church 114

The Lord Can Use Illnesses 115

We Can Shape Our Own Lives 116

The Only Way 117

You Became a Man 118

Right Now 119

Passing Through Time 120

The Outer Space of God's Love

The outer space of God's love will reach out to the end of the outer space, and you and I just don't know where it ends.

The outer space is filled with endless stars that God loves and He has given a name to them all.

The outer space has many other worlds that God's love is in where they all dwell in the outer space.

The outer space of God's love has countless galaxies that God loves and dwells in.

God loves every black hole in the outer space, where God loves to create countless new universes and give them all names.

The outer space of God's love reaches to every solar system filled with light years of God's glory, shining brighter than all the stars.

God's love is not just only here on earth, earth is only one pebble in the beach sand compared to the countless stars in the Milky Way.

We can't see the infinite outer space of God's love, because our minds can't ever comprehend it in our short lifetime here on earth.

Other worlds in the outer space can't measure God's love that is everlasting beyond the outer space.

Here on earth, prophets of God have spoken about God's love.

Pastors preach about God's love.

Poets of God write and recite about God's love.

Bible school teachers will teach about God's love.

God's musicians will sing and play music about God's love.

You and I will feel the power of God's love for believing in His Son, Jesus Christ, who is the fullness of God's love throughout the earth and throughout the outer space and throughout the highest heavens.

This world and all the other worlds can't measure the height, width and depth of God's love that overflows in the countless universes.

God is love and that is why God is God everlasting, beyond the outer space.

One day, God will destroy this sinful world out of his love that the devil and his fallen angels took for God's weakness.

God's love is eternal strength throughout the countless stars in the outer space that has an everlasting strong hold on God's love.

Let's Imagine

Let's imagine if God could have created human beings in other worlds.

Could those human beings be giants that stand at least twenty feet tall?

Could those human beings run much faster than the fastest animal in this world?

Could those human beings have wings to fly?

We just don't know what kind of creatures God could have created in other worlds.

Could those other worlds have animals?

Let's imagine if God created those other worlds to be one hundred times bigger than this world that we live in.

Could those human beings be one hundred times more intelligent than the most intelligent people here on earth?

Did those human beings not give in to any of the devil's temptations?

Could those human beings know you and me?

Can they see how we live our lives and how we treat one another?

Let's imagine if God shows those other worlds how this world has fallen into sin.

Let's imagine if God created human beings in other worlds where they may see the holy angels and talk to the holy angels all the time.

Let's imagine if those human beings talked to Jesus Christ face to face.

Could those other worlds see that we human beings fall short of God's glory?

Could those other worlds see that Jesus died for our sins on the cross?

Could those human beings in other worlds marvel at Jesus when he rose from the grave?

Let's imagine God created human beings in other worlds to one day greet us and welcome us to their worlds for being saved in Jesus Christ.

Let's imagine God created other human beings in another world, looking at us with joy when they see us going with Jesus back to heaven one day.

Could those human beings in other worlds know all those saved in Jesus or lost in their sins?

One Day There Will Be No Righteous Person On Earth

One day there will be no righteous person on earth, because Jesus Christ is coming back again to take all of His righteous children to heaven with Him.

During that time, the devil and his fallen Angels will have no one to tempt and possess on earth.

All the wicked people will be dead and there will be no living creatures on earth.

The devil and his angels will be fussing and fighting with each other, because they won't have any human being to tempt and possess on earth.

The devil and his angels will be so alone for one thousand years that the Holy Spirit will dwell with all the holy angels and all those who are saved in Jesus Christ.

Hopefully you and I will be there in heaven with all the righteous children to celebrate our victory over this sinful world.

After the thousand years is over, Jesus will bring all of his righteous children back to this world in the new Jerusalem holy city.

Jesus will raise all the wicked dead back to life.

The devil will deceive them to believe that he raised the people from the dead.

The devil will lead the charge over all the wicked people to try to attack the new Jerusalem city.

God will rain down fire and brimstone on them all and destroy the devil, his fallen angels and all the wicked people.

Jesus Christ our Lord and Savior and our God will create a new heaven and new earth for all His righteous children to live in.

The new earth will be the same earth that we are living in today, but without sin.

The earth that we are living in today is filled with so much sin.

The new earth will have no presence of sin.

You and I will be without sin in our new immortal bodies that we will live in forever and ever for being saved in Jesus Christ.

We will travel to other worlds and meet other perfect creatures that God created for His glory.

One day, there will be no righteous person on earth.

Throughout all the ages that sin has existed, it will be like a bad dream that all the righteous will wake out of when Jesus Christ comes back again to take you and me and all of His righteous children back to heaven with Him and all of His holy angels.

We will live with Jesus in the new heaven and new earth as if there was never a devil and his fallen angels trying to tempt us to sin against God.

Jesus Christ, our Lord, will surely remind us that sin existed.

We will see where the nails pierced His hands and feet and that will let us know that He gave up His life on the cross to save us from our sins.

Jesus will let us know that sin was real and not a bad dream.

One day, there will be no righteous person on earth.

The devil knows better than you and me what heaven is like, because he has been in heaven and he know that you and I and all the righteous will be so happy to be there with Jesus.

We Need to Take Jesus Christ Seriously

We can take a disappointment seriously.

We can take a heartache seriously.

We can take grieving seriously.

We can take making a mistake seriously.

We can take saying something wrong seriously.

We can take doing something wrong seriously.

We can take an illness seriously.

We can take death seriously.

We can take rejection seriously.

We can take being disrespected seriously.

We can take abuse seriously.

We can take being rude seriously.

We can take being controlling seriously.

We need to take Jesus Christ seriously to believe in Him every day.

We need to take Jesus Christ seriously for Him to save us from our sins.

We need to take Jesus Christ seriously for He can do anything but fail us.

We need to take Jesus Christ seriously for He will never leave us or forsake us.

We need to take Jesus Christ seriously for we can do all things in Jesus Christ who strengthens us.

We can take a bad habit seriously.

We can take a fault seriously.

We can take a lie seriously.

We need to take Jesus Christ seriously, for Jesus is the truth and the way and the life.

We can take bad news seriously.

We need to take Jesus Christ seriously; He is the good news to spread all around the world.

We can take falling down and hurting ourselves seriously.

We can take not finishing what we started seriously.

We can take our enemies seriously.

We need to take Jesus Christ seriously.

He overcame the world to give us the victory over our trials and temptations.

Jesus Can Use Ordinary People

Jesus can use ordinary people like me and you to spread the good news about Him to the world.

You and I don't have to be geniuses for Jesus to use us with the spiritual gifts that He gives us to build up the church.

You and I don't have to be brilliant for Jesus to use us to be a witness for Him every day.

You and I don't need a college degree for Jesus to give us His Holy Spirit.

Jesus can use ordinary people like you and me to uplift His holy and precious name.

You and I don't have to be a pastor for Jesus to use us.

You and I don't have to be an elder for Jesus to use us.

You and I don't have to be an evangelist for Jesus to use us.

You and I don't have to be a Bible school teacher for Jesus to use us.

You and I don't have to be a musician in the church for Jesus to use us.

Jesus Christ's disciples were ordinary men who Jesus used to spread the good news about Him, who is the love of God to all the world.

Jesus can use you, even if you have dropped out of high school.

Many of Jesus' disciples were ordinary people.

Many ordinary men have fought on the front lines in the battlefields.

Many ordinary men have built buildings that reached way up in the sky.

Many ordinary women have stood up for women's rights.

Many ordinary people have worked very hard to make this nation great today.

Jesus' disciples were ordinary men.

Jesus gave them the power to heal the sick and cast out demons.

Jesus can use ordinary people to do some extraordinary things.

Many educated people can be amazed to see a rich ordinary person.

Many ordinary people have good common sense to prosper in this world.

Jesus can use ordinary people every day to set the right example for educated fools who make bad choices in their lives.

Many ordinary people make good choices day after day.

Jesus can use ordinary people to win souls to be saved in Him.

Many ordinary people like me and you are saved in Jesus Christ, our Lord and Savior, who doesn't discriminate in who he saves from their sins.

Jesus also loves ordinary people who he can use to help many educated people be down to earth with their words that are not too intellectual for Jesus to understand.

The Years of Our Lives

The years of our lives are like one drop of water in the bucket of time.

We know that one drop of water can't fill up a bucket.

Time has been here on earth since the beginning of this world, but you and I haven't been here since the beginning of this world.

The years of our lives will run out and time will still exist.

We were born to live through the days, weeks, months and years that are like one drop of water in the bucket of time.

We live our lives not always realizing how fast the years are going by in our lives.

We may be so surprised today that we have aged and can't walk and run as fast as we did when we were young.

Time doesn't age as you and I live to old age.

The years of our lives are a blessing from the Lord.

So many people didn't live to reach your age or my age, even so, the years of our lives have a limit to retire us from our days on earth.

One drop of water can surely dry up in a bucket that has plenty more space for water to fill it up.

Only the Lord can give time plenty more space for other generations to come and live the years of their lives that are a blessing from the Lord who is all for us to live a long life of many years.

Everyone will not live a long life here on earth, and we do not always know why someone's life is cut short.

Many people will cut their own lives short by living a reckless lifestyle.

Even for the oldest people who ever lived on this earth, their lives were like one drop of water in the bucket of time.

They probably didn't always realize that their days, weeks, months, and years would go by so fast, like a buzzing fly flying so fast by our ears.

One drop of water can dry up fast in a big bucket.

The years of our lives can dry up so fast with old age in that big bucket of time that only the Lord can fill up with generations to come if it's in His holy will.

Only Jesus Christ, our Lord, knows the number of young people who will grow old and be like one drop of water in the bucket of time.

The Truth

How can the truth be negative, no matter what the truth is about?

The truth is always positive to let us know what is really going on.

The truth is always positive to be real with us.

How can the truth be negative if it sets us free from lies?

The truth is always positive to help us wise up.

The truth is always positive to help us do better.

How can the truth be negative and make us say something wrong?

How can the truth be negative and make us do something wrong?

The truth is always positive to convince us to say something right.

The truth is always positive to let us know how wrong we are.

The truth is always positive to let us know how right we are.

Jesus Christ is the truth and there is nothing negative about Jesus Christ.

The truth is always positive to let you and me know that we can be negative about the truth being told to us.

How can the truth be negative when somebody tells us the truth that we know is the truth?

The truth can be negative to a liar.

The truth can only be negative to someone who doesn't want to believe the truth.

The truth can only be negative to someone who doesn't like hearing the truth.

There are many church folks who don't like hearing the truth, especially if the truth is not spoken from the pastor in the church.

They believe that if you and I are not the pastor then what we say may not be the truth.

The truth can only be negative to people who run away from the truth.

The truth is always positive to anyone who loves the truth.

The truth is always positive, no matter what the truth is about.

The truth is always positive to keep us from lying to ourselves.

The truth is always positive in the Bible.

How can the truth be negative to whoever loves the truth, no matter what the truth is about and regardless of who tells the truth?

Many people don't like to hear the truth if the truth is stomping down on their guilty conscience.

Throughout the Day and Throughout the Night

Throughout the day we are very often upon our feet doing this and doing that.

We don't often think about what could go wrong, unless we are living in a warzone neighborhood.

Throughout the day, we see the sun that shines and we don't give a second thought about the sun shining down on us throughout the day.

Throughout the day, we go through the motions of doing this and doing that and we don't ask God why we must do those things because we know in our hearts that doing those things are embedded in our lives throughout the day.

Throughout the night we are very often more relaxed and much less active to lay down on our beds and go to sleep.

We need that sleep to rest our minds and bodies throughout the night that many of us will dream away throughout the night.

It is embedded in our lives because God created it to be that way.

God created the day and God created the night to be a blessing to you and me.

We are so blessed to see the day and the night that many blind people don't see and can't tell the difference between the day and night.

Throughout the day and throughout the night, God is all around us.

He gives us life that death can't wait to take away from us throughout the day and throughout the night.

Life is present throughout the day, and life is present throughout the night because of our Lord and Savior Jesus Christ, who is Lord of the day and the night.

Death is present throughout the day and death is present throughout the night because of us being born in sin to die on any day and on any night.

Throughout the day and throughout the night, Jesus truly knows what it's like to be tempted by the devil.

Throughout the day and throughout the night, Jesus knows what it's like to be hungry.

Throughout the day and throughout the night, Jesus knows what it's like to face up to death.

Throughout the day and throughout the night, Jesus knows what it's like to pray to His heavenly Father, God.

Jesus Christ, our Lord and Savior, lived here on earth so He would know what it's like to love everyone throughout the day and throughout the night.

Jesus can save us from our sins, but many people won't confess and repent throughout the day and throughout the night.

Jesus is the judge over life and death throughout the day and throughout the night.

No one can question Jesus about allowing death to come our way throughout the day and throughout the night

Jesus is in charge of all things.

Love is a Small Word

Love is a small word, but it can be really big in actions.

love is a small word, but it can be really big in justice and equality.

Love is a small word, but it can be really big in giving a helping hand.

Love is a small word, but it can be really big in a mother and a father.

Love is a small word, but it can be really big in marriage.

Love is a small word, but it can be really big in speaking the truth.

Love is a small word, but it can be really big in foster parents.

Love is a small word, but it can be really big in a sister and brother.

Love is a small word, but it can be really big in an aunt and uncle.

Love is a small word, but it can be really big in freedom.

Love is a small word, but it can be really big in a grandfather.

Love is a small word, but it can be really big in a grandmother.

Love is a small word, but it can be really big in kinfolks.

Love is a small word, but it can be really big in believing in Jesus Christ.

Love is a small word, but it can be really big in keeping God's commandments.

Love is a small word, but it can be really big in God.

Love is a small word, but it can be really big in saving lives.

Love is a small word, but it can be really big in friendships.

Love is a small word, but it can be really big in forgiveness.

Love is a small word, but it can be really big in a listening ear.

Love is a small word, but it can be really big in encouragement.

Love is a small word, but it can be really big in holding hands.

Love is a small word, but it can be really big in unity.

Love is a small word, but it can be really big in staying together.

Love is a small word, but it can be really big in hugs.

Love is a small word, but it can be really big in a relationship.

Love is a small word, but it can be really big in taking good care of your pets.

Love is a small word, but it can be really big in being selfless.

Love is a small word, but it is a really big thing in living right unto the Lord Jesus Christ.

Love is a small word, but it is a really big thing in being saved in Jesus Christ.

Love is a small word, but it is a really big thing in treating everyone right.

Jesus Was There

When we were little children, we had other children as friends who we played with while being so carefree.

When we were teenagers we had teenaged friends who we hung around with while being so carefree.

We had some friends in kindergarten, primary school, elementary school, junior high school and we had some friends in high school.

Today we are of an age where people may have lost touch with most of the friends or all of the people who we grew up with.

We may not know where they are and what they are doing if they are still alive.

Those people who were in our childhood and teenaged years passed through our lives as if we never knew them as our friends.

When we were very young children, Jesus was there with us when we just didn't know that He was there protecting us from death.

A lot of little children will die.

We don't understand why the Lord allows them to die so young.

We can believe that Jesus was there with them to give them eternal life when He comes back one day soon.

So many people have passed through our lives and we have passed through their lives, all while Jesus was there wanting to save us from our sins.

You and I can only hope that those people we grew up with are saved in Jesus Christ, if they are still alive.

If they are not alive today, we can only hope that they are saved in Jesus while sleeping in their graves.

Our dead loved ones have passed through our lives and left us with memories of them.

When they were alive in our lives, Jesus was there with them and He never left them and they were not forsaken in their ups and downs in life.

Jesus was there with us when we were very young and didn't know a lot of things as we played with other little children so carefree and not burdened with worries and uncertainties because Jesus protected us.

Jesus was there with you and me to pass us through every step of the way so that we could be here today.

Many young children will grow up to experience some of their childhood friends and teenaged friends passing through their lives for them to see that they have lost touch with some of their friends.

Jesus is there with the young children and teenagers today, just like he was there with you and me when we were little children and as we grew up to be teenagers.

We're adults today and can look back on the Lord being there with us, protecting us from death.

We just don't always know why the Lord doesn't allow all little children and teenagers to live to become adults in this world.

We can always know that Jesus was there with them, regardless of their short-lived lives.

If You and I Don't Feel Good About

If you and I don't feel good about how the Lord is blessing our brothers and sisters in the church then we're not like Jesus Christ.

You and I should be happy to see our brothers and sisters in the church doing good and well.

If our brothers and sisters in the church are joyful about sharing their spiritual gifts with you and me, we should be joyful to receive their spiritual gifts from the Lord.

We Christians, especially, should hold each other in high esteem as we are working for the Lord.

You and I should not have an "I don't care" attitude about our brothers and sisters being blessed by the Lord.

If our brothers and sisters in the church want to share their blessings with you and me, we should be eager to receive their blessings from the Lord.

It would be so great if everyone in the church was happy about their brothers and sisters growing stronger in the Lord.

You and I should be happy to see our weaker brothers and sisters growing spiritually mature in our Lord and Savior Jesus Christ, who has no favorite one who He loves the most.

Jesus loves us all in the same way, and we are equal in His holy and sinless eyesight.

If you and I don't feel good about how the Lord is blessing our brothers and sisters in the church, then we are only pretenders in the church.

If you and I don't feel good about how the Lord is blessing all of our brothers and sisters in the church, then we are spiritually dead and not spiritually alive in the Lord.

You and I should be happy for our brothers and sisters working for the

Lord,

I should be happy for you and you should be happy for me working for the Lord with eagerness to bless one another.

We don't want Jesus to say to us, "Depart from me. I never knew you who didn't love all of your brothers and sisters in the church."

We don't want Jesus to say to us, "Depart from me. I never knew you who had some brothers and sisters in the church who truly tried to reach out to you and share their spiritual gifts with you, but you just didn't feel good about accepting their spiritual gifts to help you to humble yourself."

If you and I don't feel good about how the Lord is blessing our brothers and sisters in the church, then we think too highly of ourselves and believe that we know all things and can do all things above our brothers and sisters in the church.

Only Jesus knows all things and can do all things, because He is above you and me.

The Beautiful Country

The beautiful country is good to live in.

The country roads are refreshing to drive on.

The beautiful country is so peaceful every day.

The crime rate is low in the country.

We can get a good night's sleep in the country.

Driving through the countryside can ease our minds.

The beautiful country can be so captivating to our eyes.

Living in the country can heal a broken heart.

Living in the country can heal an ill mind.

The beautiful country is a blessing from the Lord.

The Holy Spirit can speak to us even more so in the country.

The country is a quiet dwelling place for you and me to feel the presence of the Lord.

Many people love to live in the cities that can be so crowded with people.

The cities can be so noisy with traffic on the roads.

The crime rate is high in the cities.

The beautiful country can add years to our lives.

The beautiful country can help us to think right.

A lot of writers love to be in the country to gather their thoughts to write a good book.

Many people love to take their vacations to the country.

They will leave the city and go to the country to relax their mind and body.

Living in the country is like taking some good medicine to get well.

Living in the beautiful country can help us to draw closer and closer to the Lord.

The country is pretty much the safest place to live in every day.

Many people who live in the country are very down to earth people to talk to.

Many people who live in the country are friendly people.

Many people who live in the country know what it means to wait on the Lord to work things out.

Many city people are impatient and will try to work things out with their own intellect.

The beautiful country is God's marvelous handiwork.

Laws

Laws are given to us for our good.

Laws are given to us for our protection.

Laws are to be kept every day.

There are many people who love to keep the laws.

They are law abiding citizens every day.

There are many people who love to break the laws.

They just don't care to keep the laws.

Those people who love to break the laws will sooner or later end up in prison.

They will pay the price for breaking the laws.

Laws are given to us for our peace of mind.

Many people will break the laws on the highway and local roads.

They just don't care about driving over the speed limits.

They just don't care about stopping at the red lights.

They just don't care about yielding to the upcoming traffic on the roads.

Many people will plan to break the laws.

Many of the laws of men are lined up with God's holy law.

God's law is always for our good and wellbeing.

God's holy law is the highest law that all people are supposed to keep every day and every night.

There would be no prisons if everyone kept God's holy law.

There would be no murders if everyone kept God's holy law.

There would be no thieves if everyone kept God's holy law.

There would be no liars if everybody kept God's holy law.

There would be no adultery if everyone kept God's holy law.

There are people who have gotten away and never gotten caught breaking the laws of men.

No one will ever get away from God for breaking His holy law.

God is all-seeing.

No one can hide from God when they break His holy law.

The laws of men can change and some laws of men do change over time.

God's holy law will never change.

God's holy law is eternal.

Many of our government leaders will make laws, and some of them won't keep the laws that they will make.

God has never broken His own holy law.

God's holy law is His character.

Wise people will keep the laws.

Foolish people will break the laws.

In this world, there are some laws that are not good.

God's holy law is always good for us to keep every day.

Many people will know the laws of men that are not good, and that they are not good to keep.

Many good people will work hard to change those laws that are not good for the land of the living.

No one can change God's holy law and enter into heaven one day when Jesus Christ comes back again.

When Jesus lived on earth, He kept His Heavenly Father's holy law.

Keeping God's law can't save us, but it's always the right thing to do.

Jesus said that if we love Him, we will keep His commandments.

Old Sinful Ways

A lot of people will go back to their old sinful ways after the Lord has made them well from a bad illness.

A lot of people will go back to their old sinful ways after the Lord has spared their lives from death.

A lot of people will go back to their old sinful ways after the Lord has made a way for them to graduate from college and get their degree.

A lot of people will go back to their old sinful ways after the Lord has opened a door for them to get a job.

A lot of people will go back to their old sinful ways after the Lord has made a way for them to be set free from prison.

A lot of people will go back to their old sinful ways after the Lord has blessed them to start their own business.

A lot of people will pray to the Lord and ask Him to make them well again, but as soon as they get well they're right back to their old sinful ways.

A lot of people will pray to the Lord and ask Him to spare their lives, but as soon as the Lord spares their lives they are right back to their old sinful ways.

A lot of people will pray to the Lord and ask Him to make a way for them to graduate from college and get their degree, but as soon as they graduate from college and get their degree, they are right back to their old sinful ways.

A lot of people will pray to the Lord and ask Him to open a door for them to get a job, but as soon as they get the job they are right back to their old sinful ways.

A lot of people will pray to the Lord and ask Him to make a way for them to be set free from prison, but as soon as they are set free from prison they are right back to their old sinful ways.

A lot of people will pray to the Lord and ask Him to bless them to start their own business, but as soon as they start their own business they are right back to their old sinful ways.

The Lord always knows what we will do before we do it.

There is nothing that the Lord doesn't know about you and me.

The Lord knows that a lot of people will not change and live their lives unto Him after He has answered their prayers.

Is Worthy to be Worshipped

You can love your spouse, but don't worship your spouse.

You can love your children, but don't worship your children.

You can love your pets, but don't worship your pets.

You can love your friends, but don't worship your friends.

You can love your job, but don't worship your job.

You can love your house, but don't worship your house.

You can love your vehicle, but don't worship your vehicle.

You can love your career, but don't worship your career.

You can love your skills, but don't worship your skills.

You can love your talents, but don't worship your talents.

You can love your spiritual gifts, but don't worship your spiritual gifts.

You can love your parents, but don't worship your parents.

You can love your pastor but don't worship your pastor.

You can love this world, but don't worship this world.

You can love technology, but don't worship technology.

You can love science, but don't worship science.

You can love history, but don't worship history.

You can love the government, but don't worship the government.

You can love politics, but don't worship politics.

You can love nature, but don't worship nature.

You can love food, but don't worship food.

You can love the sun, but don't worship the sun.

You can love airplanes, but don't worship airplanes.

You can love the ocean, but don't worship the ocean.

You can love ships, but don't worship ships.

You can love cities, but don't worship cities.

You can love the country, but don't worship the country.

You can love people, but don't worship people.

You can love yourself, but don't worship yourself.

You can love Jesus Christ and worship Jesus Christ.

You can love Jesus Christ, who is worthy to be worshipped.

You can love Jesus Christ, who deserves to be worshipped.

You Will Never Regret It

If you give your heart to the Lord, you will never regret it.

Your heart will be made whole, no matter if you are young, middle aged or old.

Jesus Christ, the Lord, will renew your life for you to live with no regret about loving Him and obeying Him.

No one has ever regretted making their choice to deny themselves and pick up their cross to follow Jesus on the good days and on the bad days.

You will never regret it for believing in Jesus Christ.

Jesus will save you from your sins that anyone will regret for living in.

No one likes to regret anything that they say and do.

Regrets can surely cause us to feel bad.

If you give Jesus all the glory and praise, you will never regret it.

You will never regret it for being blessed by the Lord Jesus Christ.

We all love to be blessed by the Lord.

You and I will go through some trials for Jesus' name sake, but we will never regret it to receive eternal life in Jesus Christ.

You and I will never regret it for working for Jesus, because our work will never be useless in His holy eyesight.

If you put your trust in Jesus, you will never regret it because Jesus will always do what He says.

You will never regret it for keeping your eyes on Jesus.

Jesus will never deceive you for keeping your eyes on Him who will never change on you and you will know that in His holy word.

Regrets will let you and me know the mistakes that we've made.

You will never regret it for holding onto Jesus who never made a mistake and never will make a mistake.

If you humble yourself unto the Lord Jesus Christ, you will never regret it because if Jesus lifts your name up there is no telling how many people will be blessed to know your name.

If you confess and repent of your sins unto the Lord Jesus Christ, you will never regret it because Jesus will forgive you of your sins and give you a brand-new start in your life so you can live it doing His holy will.

You will never regret it for winning souls unto Jesus.

There are souls who you may never know that you led them to Jesus in your sermons, Bible school lessons, songs, poetry and with your helping hands.

Is No Competition Thing

Working for the Lord is no competition thing between one another.

Using our spiritual gifts is no competition thing, because no one's spiritual gifts are better than anyone else's spiritual gifts.

Working for the Lord is supposed to be a humble experience, so you should not be full of pride and believe that your ministry work is better than someone else's ministry work for the Lord.

We are all one body in Jesus Christ.

We all are different from one another, but no one is better than anyone else in the body of Jesus Christ.

No one should think highly of themselves if their spiritual gift is in the forefront of the church.

The Lord has given everyone a spiritual gift, even though every spiritual gift will not be so visible in the church.

Just because some spiritual gifts are not so visible does not mean that they are useless in the church.

Do not use your spiritual gifts to compete against anyone in the church.

All of God's spiritual gifts are given to us to uplift our brothers and sisters in the church.

The people of the world love to compete, especially in sports and even in the political arena where people are trying to outdo one another.

Competing against one another should never happen in the church.

Competition teaches jealousy, strife and causes divisions in the church.

The Jesus Christ that we believe in and serve is not about any kind of competition that can cause people to believe that they are superior over others.

Up in heaven, Lucifer tried to compete against God to take over God's holy throne.

Lucifer was no match for God to take God's place on his holy throne.

Competition in the church can cause people to leave the church.

Competition in the church can cause people to not love one another.

Whatever that we do for the Lord, we should do it from our hearts and not try to outshine one another in the church.

The Pharisees tried to compete against Jesus.

They believe that they were better than Jesus and tried to cause people to believe in them and to follow them in their hypocritical deeds.

Competition is all about wanting to make yourself look good.

There is no love in competition.

Our soul's salvation is no competition thing.

Jesus Christ died for us all to save us from our sins.

He rose from the grave to give us all the gift of eternal life.

No one can compete for that free gift from our Lord.

Faith in an Unseen God

Faith in an unseen God has been questioned by many people for thousands of years.

Those questions have been passed down through the ages in this world.

Many people have died with their questions not being answered.

Faith in an unseen God can be present in nature that has a Bible that is open to the world every day.

We see the sun, moon and stars that didn't create themselves.

Something has to exist above the universe.

That something that exists is unseen to us.

The Bible talks about the unseen God who sent His only begotten Son to this seen world.

Many people don't believe in the Bible or that God inspired holy men to write it.

They wrote the Bible by faith in an unseen God.

They never saw God, but they believed that God talked to them.

It's an extraordinary thing to believe in who we don't see.

It's profound to unbelievers to see you and me going to church to worship an unseen God.

They may believe that we have lost our minds because we believe in an unseen God.

Unbelievers can see that we are so different from them who live their lives by who they see and what they see.

They put their faith in visible things every day.

Faith in an unseen God is a strange thing to unbelievers.

You and I are strange to unbelievers because we have faith in an unseen God.

God is unseen but His power is seen in a nation that wins wars against unrighteous nations.

God is unseen but His glory is seen even in the beautiful rainbows that are His promise to us that there won't be another world-wide flood.

God is unseen, but His love is seen in His Son, Jesus Christ, who died on the cross to save us from our sins.

God is unseen, but His healing is seen in many sick people who get well when they should have died.

God is unseen, but His spiritual gifts are seen in the church.

God is unseen, but His blessings are seen even upon the wicked who God has no pleasure in punishing.

Faith in an unseen God will get rid of the strongholds of idol worship.

Faith in an unseen God will give strength to anyone who has faith in Him.

Without You, my Lord Jesus

Without you, my Lord Jesus, I am like a shadow that is not real.

Without you, my Lord Jesus, I am like a broken glass.

Without you, my Lord Jesus, I am like a falling star.

Without you, my Lord Jesus, I am like a big hole in a wall.

Without you, my Lord Jesus, I am like an empty box.

Without you, my Lord Jesus, I am like a frame with no picture in it.

Without you, my Lord Jesus, I am like a flat tire.

Without you, my Lord Jesus, I am like a polluted water well.

Without you, my Lord Jesus, I am like a crashed airplane.

Without you, my Lord Jesus, I am like a rusty old car.

Without you, my Lord Jesus, I am like a squeaky floor.

Without you, my Lord Jesus, I am like a dusty bookshelf.

Without you, my Lord Jesus, I am like a dead battery.

Without you, my Lord Jesus, I am nothing good.

Without you, my Lord Jesus, I am like a fogged-up window.

Without you, my Lord Jesus, I am like a rotten fruit.

Without you, my Lord Jesus, I am a mouse in a trap.

Without you, my Lord Jesus, I'm like a blank sheet of paper.

Without you, my Lord Jesus, I am like an oil spill in the ocean.

Without you, my Lord Jesus, I am like a lost house key.

Without you, my Lord Jesus, I am like a virus.

Without you, my Lord Jesus, I am like a torn shirt.

Without you, my Lord Jesus, I'm like a missing link in a chain.

Without you, my Lord Jesus, I am like a dried-up pond.

Without you, my Lord Jesus, I am like a sock with holes in it.

Without you, my Lord Jesus, I am like a trash dump.

Without you, my Lord Jesus, I am like a dirty bathtub.

Without you, my Lord Jesus, I am like a scrambled-up radio station.

Without you, my Lord Jesus, I am like a cough, spreading germs.

Without you, my Lord Jesus, I am like a scorched iron.

Without you, my Lord Jesus, I am like a bad scene.

When Jesus Lived on Earth

When Jesus lived on earth, I believe that Jesus Christ never told a lie.

I believe that Jesus always spoke the truth in love.

When Jesus lived on earth, I believe that Jesus never gossiped.

When Jesus lived on earth, I believe that Jesus never got revenge against someone else.

When Jesus lived on earth, I believe that Jesus never gave anyone an evil eye look.

When Jesus lived on earth, I believe that Jesus was never prejudiced against anyone.

When Jesus lived on earth, I believe that Jesus was never jealous of anyone.

When Jesus lived on earth, I believe that Jesus never treated anyone bad.

When Jesus lived on earth, I believed that Jesus never talked bad to anyone.

When Jesus lived on earth, I believe that Jesus never disrespected anyone.

When Jesus lived on earth, I believe that Jesus never lusted after any woman.

When Jesus lived on earth, I believe that Jesus never deceived anyone.

When Jesus lived on earth, I believe that Jesus was never proud of Himself.

When Jesus lived on earth, I believe that Jesus never hated anyone.

When Jesus lived on earth, I believe that Jesus never pretended with anyone.

When Jesus lived on earth, I believe that Jesus never sinned against God.

When Jesus lived on earth, I believe that Jesus never did anything wrong.

When Jesus lived on earth, I believe that Jesus lived without sin.

When Jesus lived on earth, I believe that Jesus never ignored anyone.

When Jesus lived on earth, I believe that Jesus never insulted anyone.

When Jesus lived on earth, I believe that Jesus never put anyone down.

When Jesus lived on earth, I believe that Jesus never wanted what belonged to someone else.

When Jesus lived on earth, I believe that Jesus never loved anyone or loved anything more than He loved his heavenly Father, God.

When Jesus lived on earth, I believe that Jesus never joked about anyone.

When Jesus lived on earth, I believe that Jesus never shamed anyone.

When Jesus lived on earth, I believe that Jesus never acted like he was better than anyone else, even though he was better than everyone else.

When Jesus lived on earth, I believe that Jesus never tried to control anyone.

When Jesus lived on earth, I believe that Jesus never made a mistake.

When Jesus lived on earth, I believe that Jesus never despised anyone.

When Jesus lived on earth, I believe that Jesus never talked bad about anyone behind their backs.

When Jesus lived on earth, I believe that Jesus never had any unnatural affections.

When Jesus lived on earth, I believe that Jesus never had any bad motives.

When Jesus lived on earth, I believe that Jesus never had any bad intentions.

When Jesus lived on earth, I believe that Jesus never abused anyone.

When Jesus lived on earth, I believe that Jesus never abandoned anyone.

When Jesus lived on earth, I believe that Jesus never changed on anyone.

When Jesus lived on earth, I believe that Jesus was a perfect man without sin in His flesh.

I believe that Jesus Christ is the Son of God.

How We are Raised Up

How we are raised can surely mold us and shape our lives.

If we are raised in a loving family it can surely help us to be loving people and do our neighbors good.

If we are raised in a hateful family, it can surely cause us to be hateful people and do our neighbors bad.

How we are raised can surely show and tell in our lives.

If we are raised in a family that loves to gossip, it can surely cause us to love to gossip about other people.

If we are raised in a family that loves to tell lies, it can surely cause us to love to tell lies.

If we are raised in a family that has a lot of pride, it can surely cause us to have a lot of pride.

If we are raised in a family that believes they are better than others, it can surely cause us to believe that we are better than others.

Whoever confesses and repents of their sins unto Jesus Christ and gets baptized will become a part of a spiritual family.

We are raised in a spiritual family to be like Jesus Christ, who will surely renew our lives for us to love and cause us to love one another.

If we live for Jesus, He will raise us up spiritually and we will humble ourselves before Him.

If we live for Jesus, He will raise us up spiritually for us to deny oneself and pick up our cross and follow him.

If we live for Jesus, He will raise us up spiritually for us to obey him.

If we live for Jesus, He will raise us up spiritually for us to be a witness for Him.

If we live for Jesus, He will raise us up spiritually for us to give testimonies about Him.

If we live for Jesus, He will raise us up spiritually for us to be willing to die for His holy namesake.

Being raised up spiritually by Jesus Christ will never burden us or bring us down.

Being raised up spiritually by Jesus Christ will surely bless our lives.

Being raised up spiritually by Jesus Christ will surely cause our old sinful selves to leave us.

Love is Every Good Thing

Love is every good thing to make this a better world.

Education is not every good thing — there are a lot of educated fools.

Beauty is not every good thing — there are a lot of selfish beautiful women.

Love is every good thing to always hold onto.

Technology is not every good thing — many people will use technology to do evil things.

Talents are not every good thing — many people are talented but have bad motives.

Love is every good thing to always be trusted.

Intelligence is not every good thing — many people will use their intelligence to deceive people.

Medicine is not every good thing — people are taking too much medicine that makes them more worse off than what they were before they took the medicine.

Love is every good thing.

Love is God, who is every good thing.

Skills are not every good thing — many people are skillful at making people look bad.

Money is not every good thing — many people will waste their money buying things that they don't need.

Love is every good thing.

God so loved the world that He gave us His only begotten Son that whoever so believe in Him shall not perish but will have eternal life.

Human Reasoning

Human reasoning will cause us to boast about ourselves.

Human reasoning will cause us to make a lot of mistakes.

Human reasoning will cause us to put our trust in this world.

Human reasoning will cause us to love the creature more than the creator, God.

Human reasoning will cause us to get in some trouble.

Human reasoning will cause us to disregard God's holy word.

Human reasoning will cause us to do our own will.

Human reasoning will take us to a fall.

Human reasoning will cause arguments.

Human reasoning will cause riots.

Human reasoning will cause wars.

If our reasoning is about loving and obeying the Lord, we will have peace of mind in this world when things are going bad.

Human reasoning will cause us to believe what is not true.

Human reasoning will cause us to give up on our loved ones who have turned their backs on our Lord Jesus Christ.

Human reasoning will cause us to believe that our problems are bigger than Jesus.

Human reasoning will cause us to not turn the other cheek if somebody does us wrong.

Human reasoning will cause us to get deceived by the things of the world.

If our reasoning is to trust the Lord, we won't be swept under the rug of being disappointed by the people of the world.

Human reasoning will cause us to take our eyes off of Jesus and look at the awards, achievements, honors and heroic deeds in this world that will one day pass away.

Human reasoning will cause us to believe that we made ourselves talented and skillful and educated and successful.

If our reasoning is to give Jesus Christ all the credit for everything, then we should know that we can't do anything good without Him allowing us to do good things.

To Accept

You want people to accept your sermons.

You want people to accept what you teach.

You want people to accept the songs that you sing.

You want people to accept your talents.

You want people to accept your skills.

You want people to accept your dreams.

You want people to accept what you say.

You want people to accept what you do.

Everyone in this world wants to be accepted.

A liar wants people to accept his or her lies.

A fool wants people to accept his or her foolishness.

You want people to accept you whether you're right or wrong.

You want people to accept you whether you're good or bad.

You want people to accept your intelligence.

You want people to accept your education.

you want people to accept your common sense.

You want people to accept your advice.

You want people to accept your rules.

You want people to accept your life.

You want people to accept your ministry.

Who doesn't want to be accepted?

Jesus Christ, our Lord, wants to be accepted by sinners like you and me.

Jesus Christ, our Lord and Savior, wants to be accepted in everyone's life.

Jesus Christ wants everyone to accept His salvation.

Even an evil person wants his or her evil words to be accepted.

Even an evil person wants his or her evil deeds to be accepted.

Jesus Christ, our Lord and Savior, wants everyone to accept His saving grace.

Jesus Christ, our Lord and Savior, wants everyone to accept His holy word.

Jesus Christ, our Lord and Savior, wants everyone to accept His commandments.

Jesus Christ, our Lord and Savior, wants everyone to accept the truth.

You want people to accept you for who you are.

You want people to accept the color of your skin.

Jesus Christ, our Lord and Savior, wants everyone to accept Him in this life.

In this life is the time to accept him and be saved — it will be too late to accept Him after we die.

If we don't accept Jesus Christ as our Lord and Savior before we die, then Jesus Christ won't accept us on His clouds of glory when He comes back again.

You Can Put Your Belief in Jesus Christ

You can put your belief in Jesus Christ, who is perfect without sin to never make a mistake.

Jesus will never say anything wrong or do anything wrong, so you can put your belief in Jesus Christ each and every day for the rest of your life.

Jesus will never fail you.

Jesus will never leave you or forsake you.

Jesus will never lie to you.

Jesus will never deceive you.

Jesus will never stop loving you.

You can't put your belief in yourself, because you will make some mistakes.

You can't put your belief in yourself, because you will say something wrong.

You can't put your belief in yourself, because you will fail at something.

You can put your belief in Jesus Christ who is all-knowing.

You can put your belief in Jesus Christ who is all-wise.

You can put your belief in Jesus Christ who is all-powerful.

You can put your belief in Jesus Christ who is all-loving.

You can put your belief in Jesus Christ who is all-fair.

You can't put your belief in any man, woman, boy or girl.

No man, woman, boy or girl is all-knowing.

No man, woman, boy or girl is all-wise.

No man, woman, boy or girl is all-powerful.

No man, woman, boy or girl is perfect without sin.

No man, woman, boy or girl will say all the right words.

No man, woman, boy or girl will do all the right things.

No man, woman, boy or girl is all-victorious.

You can't put your belief in any man, woman, boy or girl because they will make some mistakes.

You can put your belief in Jesus Christ who is all-victorious.

You can't put your belief in any man, woman, boy or girl who is not all-loving.

You can put your belief in Jesus Christ for as long as you live.

You can't put your belief in any man, woman, boy or girl who can change on you.

You can put your belief in Jesus Christ who will never change on you.

Jesus is the same yesterday, today and tomorrow, and you can put your belief in Jesus Christ.

It's Good to Love Everyone

It's good to love everyone, but it's not good to let people use you.

It's good to love everyone, but it's not good to let people abuse you.

It's good to love everyone, but it's not good to gossip with people.

It's good to love everyone, but it's not good to keep company with bad people.

It is good to love everyone, but it's not good to let people cause you to do evil things.

It's good to love everyone, but it's not good to let people bring you down to nothing good.

It's good to love everyone, but it's not good to let people cause you to lose your faith in the Lord Jesus Christ.

It's good to love everyone, but it's not good to let people cause you to turn your back on Jesus.

It's good to love everyone, but it's not good to let people cause you to sin against God.

It's good to love everyone, but it's not good to let people cause you to not be saved in Jesus Christ.

It's good to love everyone, but it's not good to let people control you.

It's good to love everyone, but it's not good to let people walk all over you.

It's good to love everyone, but it's not good to let people change your mind from doing something good.

It's good to love everyone, but it's not good to let people put you down.

It's good to love everyone, but it's not good to let people cause you to get angry and do something wrong.

It's good to love everyone, but it's not good to let people push you around.

It's good to love everyone, but it's not good to let people cause you to not confess and repent of your sins to the Lord.

It's good to love everyone, but it's not good to let people cause you to be lost in your sins.

It's good to love everyone, but it's not good to let people cause you to not go to church and worship the Lord.

A New Day May Be

A new day may be a happy day to someone.
A new day may be a sad day to someone.
A new day may be a peaceful day to someone.
A new day may be a confusing day to someone.
A new day may be a memorable day to someone.
A new day may be a freedom day to someone.
A new day may be a dreadful day to someone.
A new day may be a burdensome day to someone.
A new day may be a grieving day to someone.
A new day may be a boring day to someone.
A new day may be a prosperous day to someone.
A new day may be a frightening day to someone.
A new day may be a challenging day to someone.
Any new day may be a doom day to someone.
A new day may be a celebration day to someone.
A new day may be a terrible day to someone.
A new day may be a glorious day to someone.
A new day may be a quiet day to someone.
A new day may be a rewarding day to someone.
A new day may be a mysterious day to someone.
A new day may be a very good day to someone.
A new day may be an unpredictable day to someone.
A new day may be a confession day to someone.
A new day may be a repenting day to someone.

A new day may be a day of thanks unto the Lord for someone.

Every new day is a day of thanksgiving unto the Lord.

Every new day is a day of living our lives unto the Lord.

Every new day is a day of having faith in the Lord.

Every new day is a day of giving the Lord all the glory and praise.

Every new day is a day of being saved in our Lord Jesus Christ.

Have Sense Enough to Know

Many people have sense enough to know that they are treated right.

Many people have sense enough to know that they are treated bad.

many people have sense enough to know that they said something wrong.

Many people have sense enough to know that they have done something wrong.

Many people have sense enough to know that something is not right.

Many people have sense enough to know that something doesn't sound right.

Many people have sense enough to know what is right.

Many people have sense enough to know what is wrong.

Many people have sense enough to know if you and I are real with them.

Many people have sense enough to know if you and I love them.

Many people have sense enough to know what they can do.

Many people have sense enough to know who they are.

And many people have sense enough to know what they believe.

Many people have sense enough to know if you and I are telling them the truth.

Many people have sense enough to know if you and I are telling them a lie.

Many people have sense enough to know if they are well.

Many people have sense enough to know if they are sick.

Many people have sense enough to know if they are good.

Many people have sense enough to know if they are evil.

Many people have sense enough to know that they are no better than anyone else.

Many people have sense enough to know they are not perfect.

Many people have sense enough to know if their lives are in danger.

Many people have sense enough to know that they don't know everything.

Many people have sense enough to know that they can't do everything.

Many people have sense enough to know that they have done something bad.

Many people have sense enough to know that they have done something good.

Many people have sense enough to know if they've told a lie.

Many people have sense enough to know if they have told the truth.

Many people have sense enough to know that there is a God.

Many people have sense enough to know that the Bible is true.

Many people have sense enough to know there is only one Lord and Savior, Jesus Christ.

Death Doesn't Care About

Death doesn't care about how brilliant you are.

Death doesn't care about how happy you are.

Death doesn't care about how heroic you are.

Death doesn't care about how good you are.

Death doesn't care about how bad you are.

Death doesn't care about how foolish you are.

Death doesn't care about how wise you are.

Death doesn't care about how young you are.

Death doesn't care about how old you are.

Death doesn't care about how rich you are.

Death doesn't care about how poor you are.

Death doesn't care about how many awards you have.

death doesn't care about how famous you are.

Death doesn't care about how great you are.

Death doesn't care about the color of your skin.

Death doesn't care about how healthy you are.

Death doesn't care about how many lives you saved.

Death doesn't care about how many college degrees you have.

death doesn't care about how many skills you have.

death doesn't care about how many talents you have.

Death doesn't care about you being married.

Death doesn't care about you being single.

Death doesn't care about you being a Christian.

Death doesn't care about you not being a Christian.

Death doesn't care about how beautiful you look.

Death doesn't care about how strong you are.

Jesus Christ, the Lord, got the victory over death when He arose from the grave.

Jesus will give you and me the victory over death when He comes back again to give us eternal life for being saved in Him.

Jesus cares about us all and wants to save us all from being lost in our sins before we die.

Man Can't Tame the Tongue

Man can tame a dog.

Man can tame a bear.

Man can tame a lion.

Man can't tame the tongue.

Man can tame a tiger.

Man can tame a whale.

Man can tame a dolphin.

Man can't tame the tongue.

Man can tame a leopard.

Man can tame a goat.

Man can tame a bull.

Man can't tame the tongue.

Man can tame a ram.

Man can tame a moose.

Man can tame a horse.

Man can't tame the tongue.

Man can tame a giraffe.

Man can tame an eagle.

Man can tame a hawk.

Man can't tame the tongue.

Man can tame an elephant.

Man can tame a buffalo.

Man can tame a kangaroo.

Man can't tame the tongue.

Man can tame a fox.

Man can tame a camel.

Man can tame a wolf.

Man can't tame the tongue.

Man can tame a gorilla.

Man can tame a monkey.

Man can tame a rhino.

Man can't tame the tongue.

Man can tame a pig.

Man can tame a seal.

Man can't tame the tongue.

The tongue can be like a poisonous snake that man can't tame.

Don't Look at Other People

Don't look at other people's flaws when Jesus wants you to keep your eyes on Him who never had a one flaw.

Don't look at other people's mistakes when Jesus wants you to keep your eyes on Him who never made a mistake.

Don't look at other people's bad habits when Jesus wants you to keep your eyes on Him who never had a bad habit.

Don't look at other people's wrongdoings when Jesus wants you to keep your eyes on Him who never did anything wrong.

Don't look at other people's problems when Jesus wants you to keep your eyes on Him who never had any problems.

Don't look at other people's sins when Jesus wants you to keep your eyes on Him who never sinned against God when He lived on earth without sin in His words and flesh.

Don't look at other people's failures when Jesus wants you to keep your eyes on Him who cannot fail you and me.

Other people can't work out your soul's salvation.

Other people can't cleanse you from your sins.

Other people can't save you from your sins.

Other people can't pick up your cross for you.

Other people don't have a heaven to put you in.

Only Jesus Christ can cleanse you of your sins.

Only Jesus can save you from our sins.

Only Jesus can give you salvation.

Only Jesus Christ has a heaven to put you in.

Convicted

We don't usually like to be convicted of thinking something wrong.

We don't usually like to be convicted of saying something wrong.

We don't usually like to be convicted of doing something wrong.

We have a sinful nature that can deceive us into believing that we are so right in our own eyes all of the time.

If we have the Holy Spirit, we will be convicted if we think something wrong.

If we have the Holy Spirit, we will be convicted of saying something wrong.

If we have the Holy Spirit, we will be convicted of doing something wrong.

If we never ever feel convicted about anything in our hearts, then we don't have the Holy Spirit dwelling in us.

Many people will reject being convicted of their wrongdoings.

They are truly rejecting the Holy Spirit who convicts us all of our sins.

No one in this world is without sin to never be convicted of saying something wrong and doing something wrong.

We are all guilty in the presence of the Lord Jesus Christ, who will forgive us of our sins if we confess and repent.

No Christian is too righteous and holy to never be convicted by the Holy Spirit.

Conviction is always a good thing to let you and me know that only Jesus Christ is worthy to get all the glory and all the praise every day.

Conviction lets us know that we are all sinners saved through Jesus' grace.

Conviction lets us know that we are no better than anyone else.

Conviction lets us know that we fall short of the glory of God.

Conviction lets us know that we all need Jesus Christ to cleanse us and save us from our sins.

If we never feel conviction about anything in our hearts, then the Holy Spirit is not in us, regardless of holding positions in the church.

If we never feel convicted about anything in our hearts, then the Holy Spirit is not in us, regardless of good works that we do.

If we never feel convicted in our hearts, then the Holy Spirit is not in us, regardless of looking like a Christian in the eyes of others.

Conviction lets us know that we need to repent of our sins.

We all have some sins to repent of.

Some of us have more sins than others to repent of unto the Lord.

Conviction will set us free from believing that we're perfect in our own eyes.

You Shouldn't Let It Go to Your Head

If the Lord blesses you to get a good job, you shouldn't let it go to your head.

If the Lord blesses you to get a college degree, you shouldn't let it go to your head.

If the Lord blesses you to be a pastor, you shouldn't let it go to your head.

If the Lord blesses you to be a computer genius, you shouldn't let it go to your head.

if the Lord blesses you to be an engineer you, shouldn't let it go to your head.

If the Lord blesses you to be an aircraft pilot you, shouldn't let it go to your head.

If the Lord blesses you to be a tractor trailer truck driver, you shouldn't let it go to your head.

If the Lord blesses you to be a policeman you, shouldn't let it go to your head.

If the Lord blesses you to be a firefighter you, shouldn't let it go to your head.

If the Lord blesses you to be a marine you, shouldn't let it go to your head.

If the Lord blesses you to be a Navy SEAL, you shouldn't let it go to your head.

If the Lord blesses you to be a senator, you shouldn't let it go to your head.

If the Lord blesses you to have your own business, you shouldn't let it go to your head.

If the Lord blesses you to be a school teacher, you shouldn't let it go to your head.

If the Lord blesses you to be a doctor, you shouldn't let it go to your head.

If the Lord blesses you to be a president of the United States, you shouldn't let it go to your head.

If the Lord blesses you to be a scientist, you shouldn't let it go to your head.

If the Lord blesses you to be a news journalist, you should not let it go to your head.

If the Lord blesses you to get rich, you shouldn't let it go to your head.

If the Lord blesses you to look beautiful, you shouldn't let it go to your head.

If the Lord blesses you to be a great athlete, you shouldn't let it go to your head.

If the Lord blesses you to be a hero, you shouldn't let it go to your head.

If the Lord blesses you to be a great writer, you shouldn't let it go to your head.

If the Lord blesses you to be a missionary, you shouldn't let it go to your head.

If the Lord blesses you to be a judge, you shouldn't let it go to your head.

If the Lord blesses you to be a racecar driver, you shouldn't let it go to your head.

If the Lord blesses you to be a college professor, you shouldn't let it go to your head.

If the Lord blesses you to be an editor, you shouldn't let it go to your head.

If the Lord blesses you to be a musician, you shouldn't let it go to your head.

If the Lord blesses you to be a movie star, you shouldn't let it go to your head.

If the Lord blesses you to climb the highest mountain, you shouldn't let it go to your head.

If the Lord blesses you to be a lion tamer, you shouldn't let it go to your head.

If the Lord blesses you to walk on a tight wire across the Grand Canyon, you shouldn't let it go to your head.

The Lord giveth and the Lord can take it away from you and me.

Pride will sooner or later take you and me to a fall.

You and I must keep ourselves humble before the Lord.

Uncomfortable

If we are not living right, the truth can make us feel uncomfortable.

Someone can say something and make us feel uncomfortable.

Someone can do something and make us feel uncomfortable.

Someone can stare at us and make us feel uncomfortable.

There are church folks who can make us feel uncomfortable.

Jesus Christ, our Lord, must have felt uncomfortable when the Pharisees tried to trap Him into saying something wrong.

If you and I feel uncomfortable when someone tells us the truth, especially about God's holy word, then we are guilty of doing something wrong.

It is a good thing that the truth can make us feel uncomfortable, because it lets us know that we need to confess and repent of our sins.

There are some moments in the church when you and I can feel uncomfortable about not being loved by everyone in the church.

Telling people the truth can make them feel uncomfortable if they don't like the truth being told to them.

The truth will make you and me comfortable if we love hearing the truth and love living the truth.

There are some church folks who will feel so comfortable about showing more love to those who are educated in the church.

There are some church folks who will feel so comfortable about believing that they are better than others in the church.

There are some church folks who will feel so comfortable with making assumptions about others in the church.

You and I should feel uncomfortable about loving some church folks more than others in the church.

You and I should feel uncomfortable about believing that we are better than others in the church.

You and I should feel uncomfortable with making assumptions about others in the church.

If we feel uncomfortable about those things, then we are surely walking on the straight and narrow path of discipleship.

There are people who will feel uncomfortable with love.

They've been treated bad so much in their life that they do not know what love is.

They may feel more comfortable with violence and contention.
Jesus says, "You are My disciples if you have love for one another."

If Being Black is a Crime

If being black is a crime then God, Himself, committed a crime for creating black men, women, boys and girls.

Many people believe that all black people are criminals living among them day after day.

How can it be a crime to be black when God has blessed many black people to get a good education?

How can it be a crime to be black when God has blessed many black people to be great athletes?

How can it be a crime to be black when we had a black president?

How can it be a crime to be black when there is a black woman vice president?

How can it be a crime to be black when there are black judges?

How can it be a crime to be black when there are black doctors?

How can it be a crime to be black when there are black surgeons?

God didn't commit a crime when He created a black man like me.

How can it be a crime to be black when there are black scientists?

How can it be a crime to be black when there are black mayors?

How can it be a crime to be black when there are black movie stars?

How can it be a crime to be black when there are black police officers and chiefs of police?

How can it be a crime to be black when there are black gymnasts?

No one can accuse God of committing a crime for creating black men, women, boys and girls in His image.

No one can arrest God for creating black people.

No one can handcuff God for creating black people.

No one can shoot God for creating black people.

No one can put a chokehold on God for creating black people.

No one can lock God up in jail for creating black people.

No one can give God a lifetime sentence for creating black people.

So how can it be a crime to be black when there are black preachers?

How can it be a crime to be black when there are black school teachers?

How can it be a crime to be black when there are black nurses?

How can it be a crime to be black when there are black college professors?

How can it be a crime to be black when there are black ballet dancers?

How can it be a crime to be black when there are black mechanics?

How can it be a crime to be black when there are black social workers?

How can it be a crime to be black when there are black engineers?

How can it be a crime to be black when there are black millionaires and billionaires?

If being black is a crime, then God would only allow black murderers to get the death penalty.

God, Himself, will make sure that white people see His wrath upon only black murderers.

How can it be a crime to be black when there are black soldiers who fought in wars so that we can live our lives in freedom?

How can it be a crime to be black when there are black senators speaking out for equality and justice for all people in this great nation?

How can it be a crime to be black when there are black news journalists?

How can it be a crime to be black when there are black chefs who can cook some of the best meals in this world?

How can it be a crime to be black when many black people are the best employers on their jobs?

God created wonderfully made black people, just like He did every other race of people.

If being black is a crime, then God would only judge black people, but that's so not true of what God would do.

If being black is a crime God would not even allow a dog to live with black people.

If being black is a crime, then God wouldn't allow a white man or white woman to go to prison for committing a crime.

How can it be a crime to be black when there are black artists?

If being black is a crime, then God would be an unjust God.

If being black is a crime, then God would sentence every black man, woman, boy and girl to burn in hell.

If being black is a crime, then Jesus would have left black people out of His saving grace.

Jesus would not have died for the sins of black people.

If being black is a crime, then Jesus will not take any black person to heaven with Him when He comes back again.

If being black is a crime, then why would black people even exist?

God created black people to exist in this old world.

How can it be a crime to be black when there are black military officers?

How can it be a crime to be black when there are black real estate agents?

How can it be a crime to be black when there are black-owned businesses?

How can it be a crime to be black when there are black aircraft pilots?

How can it be a crime to be black when there are black Christians?

If being black is a crime, then God would only allow black people to be locked up in prison.

Being black is no crime to God, even though it seems that being black is a crime to many people of another race.

They might look at being black as a threat to them, and they won't trust anyone who is black.

If being black is a crime, then God would had never created black people to live in this world.

If being black is a crime, then God owes it to every black man, woman, boy and girl to tell us why we are criminals.

If being black is a crime, then all of us black people would be criminals in God's eyesight.

If being black is a crime, then God would allow the ignorance of other races of people to be the right thing to judge black people every day.

Being black is no crime to God, who can heal our wounds of inequality, segregation, discrimination, injustice and oppression that's been going on for hundreds of years.

One day soon, Jesus Christ will come back again and put an end to all of this racism and racists will burn in hell.

Racism is a criminal to God every day.

How can it be a crime to be black when there are black firefighters?

How can it be a crime to be black when there are black carpenters?

Being black is no crime to God, but being black is a crime to anyone who is prejudiced against black people.

God didn't commit a crime when He created black people to live in this world.

We black people are under the microscope of injustice that makes all of us look like we were born in this world to be only criminals.

If being black is a crime, then God would not have allowed black people to integrate with other cultures of people.

Being black is no crime to God, who doesn't love any other race of people more than He loves us black people.

Believe

Many people believe that magic can make them do extraordinary things.

Many people believe in luck to save their lives.

Many people believe in witchcraft to get them everything that they want.

Many people believe that they can talk to their dead loved ones.

Many people believe that education can make them do all things.

Many people believe that money can take away all of their problems.

Many people believe the horoscopes will lead them to their soulmate.

Many people believe the government will make all the right laws.

Many people believe the Pope speaks as God.

Many people believe their jobs will make them secure.

Many people believe that they are right about everything they say.

Many people believe they are better than you and me.

Many people believe they can't do anything wrong.

Many people believe they know everything.

Many people believe they can do anything.

Many people believe in medicine to cure them from every illness.

Many people believe in man to give them hope in this unstable world.

Many people believe in technology to make this world last forever.

The greatest belief is believing in Jesus Christ, who is the Son of God.

That is the only belief that will never fail anyone in this world.

Don't Put Off

Don't put off doing something good today, because another day is not promised to you and me.

So, do something good for yourself or someone else, and most of all, do something good in the name of the Lord.

Don't put off doing something good this week, because another week is not promised to you and me.

Do something good that someone else can be blessed by.

Don't put off doing something good this month, because another month is not promised to you and me.

Do something good you won't regret.

Don't put off doing something good this year, because another year is not promised to you and me to do something good that someone may never forget.

Jesus Christ doesn't put off one second, one minute and one hour to want to save us from our sins because he loves us with an everlasting love.

A Loan from God

Your life is a loan from God.

Your health is a loan from God.

Your strength is a loan from God.

Your house is a loan from God.

Your pets are a loan from God.

Your education is a loan from God.

Your talents are a loan from God.

Your skills are a loan from God.

Your clothes are a loan from God.

Your shoes are a loan from God.

Your wife is a loan from God.

Your husband is a loan from God.

Your children are a loan from God.

Your grandchildren are a loan from God.

Your retirement is a loan from God.

Your retirement checks are a loan from God.

Your checking account is a loan from God.

Your savings account is a loan from God.

Your Social Security checks are a loan from God.

Your mother is a loan from God.

Your father is a loan from God.

Your sisters are a loan from God.

Your brothers are a loan from God.

Your friends are a loan from God.

Your family is a loan from God.

Your church family is a loan from God.

You and me don't own anything.

All that we have is a loan from God.

Our mind and body are a loan from God.

There is No Retirement in Jesus Christ

You can retire from your job.

You can retire from being a pastor at a church.

You can retire from the military.

There is no retirement in Jesus Christ.

You can't retire from praying to Jesus.

You can't retire from having faith in Jesus.

You can't retire from trusting in Jesus.

There is no retirement in Jesus Christ.

You can't retire from loving Jesus Christ.

You can't retire from loving your neighbors.

You can't retire from keeping God's commandments.

There is no retirement in Jesus Christ, the Son of God.

You can't retire from denying yourself and picking up your cross to follow Jesus.

You can't retire from living your life unto Jesus Christ.

There is no retirement for you and me when it comes to being saved in Jesus Christ.

In God We Trust

In God we trust — we trust in His holy begotten Son, Jesus Christ, who gave up His life to save us from our sins with the price that He paid.

In God we trust — we trust in His love for all of us who can choose to believe in His son before we go back to the dust of the earth.

In God we trust — we trust Him who gave us His Son to crush the serpent's head from poisoning our souls with his sins that we must confess and repent of unto Jesus Christ.

In God we trust — we trust God to give us an A+ on the test of life for loving and obeying His Son, Jesus Christ, who is our best teacher of the renewed life that we live unto Him.

In God we trust — we trust God to never fuss at us for sinning against Him.

In God we Trust — we trust God who gave us His Son who will never leave us hanging on the limb of life when we deny ourselves and pick up our crosses and follow him.

Jesus Always Cares

Jesus always cares about how we feel, even when no one else may care about how we feel.

Jesus will always come for us and give us the answer to how we feel.

Jesus always cares about us when we get sick.

Jesus always cares enough about us to make us well, even if the doctor may believe that it is impossible for us to get well.

Jesus is a miracle worker — He can make us feel well even if the doctor gives up on us.

If it is in Jesus' holy will for us to get well, we will get well.

Jesus always cares about how we live our lives day after day.

Jesus doesn't want us to live a dangerous life, doing foolish things that can shorten our lives.

Jesus always cares about our life, health and strength.

Jesus wants us to live a long life in His will.

If we live a short life, it may not be our fault, but the Lord always cares enough to give us eternal life if we are saved in Him.

Jesus Christ, our Lord and Savior, always cares about you and me and He will never give up on us, even if we give up on Him.

If we don't always care to love and keep His commandments, Jesus will still always care about what we go through.

He will be there for us to carry us through our misfortunes in life, if we choose to let Him into our hearts and allow Him to dwell in us.

Jesus always cares to save us from our sins before we die.

Jesus Has His

Jesus has His genius Christians who He uses to reach out to other genius people with the gospel about Him who saves sinners.

Jesus has His brilliant Christians who He uses to reach out to other brilliant people with the gospel about Him who saves sinners.

Jesus has His intellectual Christians who He uses to reach out to other intellectual people with the gospel about Him who saves sinners.

Jesus has His smart Christians who He uses to reach out to other smart people with the gospel about Him who saves sinners.

Jesus has His common-sense Christians who he uses to reach out to other common-sense people with the gospel about Him who saves sinners.

Jesus Christ, our Lord and Savior, is all-wise.

He stays ahead of all of us and knows what to do to save sinners like you and me.

The gospel of Jesus Christ will be spread throughout the world by we Christians who are on different levels of education, which allows us to reach out to everyone in this world with the gospel.

Jesus has His faithful and obedient Christians on every level, and they are communicating the gospel good news about Him who saves sinners from being lost in sin.

The Partly Cloudy Days in Our Lives

The clouds up in the sky can look so beautiful on a partly cloudy day.

The sun will radiate through the clouds on a partly cloudy day.

On a partly cloudy day, the clouds can look so uniform up in the sky all day long.

The clouds can stand at attention and salute on a partly cloudy day, and the sun will shine its light through the clouds.

Our moments in the day can be partly good and partly bad.

On a partly cloudy day, the clouds can't cover up the whole sky.

The partly cloudy days of our lives can't cover up all of our blessings from the Lord.

We can surely thank the Lord all the days in our lives are not covered up with clouds of disappointment.

We can surely thank the Lord that all the days in our lives are not covered up with clouds of uncertainty.

We can surely thank the Lord that all the days in our lives are not covered up with clouds of doubt and clouds of fear.

The partly cloudy days of our lives can surely be a blessing to us, because they let us know that the Lord can shine a way out of no way through the partly cloudy days of our lives for us to be blessed by Him.

You Know What it Will Take

Oh Lord, You know what it will take for me to keep my faith in You.

Oh Lord, You know what it will take for me to keep my trust in You.

Oh Lord, You know what it will take for me to hold on to You.

Oh Lord, You know what it will take for me to keep myself humble unto You.

Oh Lord, You know what it will take for me to keep on loving You.

Oh Lord, You know what it will take for me to keep on obeying You.

Oh Lord, You know what it will take to save me from being lost in my sins.

There are People Who Believe

There are people who believe that they are so spiritual and high up in the Lord.

They believe that they are too high up to be blessed by your ministry work and my ministry work for the Lord.

There are people who believe that they are so high up in favor from the Lord.

They believe that you and I have no good favor with the Lord because we may not have the spiritual gifts that they have in the church.

There are people who believe that they are so high up in their relationship with the Lord, and they believe that you and I don't have a relationship with the Lord.

There are people who believe that they are so in touch with the Lord.

They believe that you and I are out of touch with the Lord because we may not be articulate like them when it comes to praying to the Lord.

There are people who believe that they are so faithful to the Lord, but they do not believe what you and I are doing for the Lord.

There are people who believe that they are so close to the Lord.

They believe that you and I are not close to the Lord because they may not see a big change in our lives.

There are people who believe that they are so righteous in the Lord.

They believe that you and I are not righteous enough because they may see you and me do something wrong.

There will always be those people who believe that they are called by the Lord to do great things in His holy name.

They believe that you and I may not be called by the Lord to do great things in His holy and precious name.

Will Obey Jesus

The sun will obey Jesus and shine all day long.

The moon will obey Jesus and glow all night long.

The stars will obey Jesus and sparkle all night long.

The night will obey Jesus and be dark all night long.

The grass will obey Jesus and cover the ground every day.

The trees will obey Jesus and stand up on its roots every day.

The trees will obey Jesus and cover the earth every day.

The River will obey Jesus and follow into the ocean every day.

The oceans will obey Jesus and cover three quarters of the earth every day.

The ground will obey Jesus and hold together for you and me.

The sky will obey Jesus and hover over us every day.

The rainbows will obey Jesus and give us their sign that there will be no more worldwide flood.

So many people will not obey Jesus because they just don't want to obey Jesus.

God didn't create nature in His image, even though nature seems to be wiser than many people who are not wise for disobeying Jesus Christ, our Lord.

Failures

Your failures can be made into triumphs if you give your failures to the Lord.

There is nothing too hard for the Lord to do for you.

The Lord can do anything but fail you.

The Lord Jesus Christ is all-victorious and will take all of your failures and cast them in the bottom of the deepest ocean.

Your failures can be made into a learning experience if you give your failures to Jesus Christ, the Lord who has no failures in His holy name.

Jesus never failed at doing anything from His childhood to His manhood.

Jesus never failed at His words and deeds that were all-victorious when He lived here on earth.

Everyone was born in sin and will fail in something.

You and I fall short of the glory of God.

Only Jesus can always use our failures to help us to wise up and not make the same mistakes over and over again.

Failures are like a wound to our souls.

Jesus can surely heal our souls if we give our failures to Him.

He will surprise us with what He can do with our failures.

Only Jesus can make our failures change us so we can do so much better in life.

The Right Thing to Do

Getting married is the right thing to do.

Fornicating is not the right thing to do.

Telling the truth is the right thing to do.

Telling lies is not the right thing to do.

Getting an education is the right thing to do.

Dropping out of school is not the right thing to do.

Getting a job is the right thing to do.

Being lazy is not the right thing to do.

Talking to the person who offended you is the right thing to do.

Talking to others behind their backs is not the right thing to do.

Loving our neighbors is the right thing to do.

Hating people is not the right thing to do.

Going to church is the right thing to do.

Staying home and away from church is not the right thing to do.

Loving and obeying Jesus Christ is the right thing to do.

Rejecting Jesus Christ is not the right thing to do.

Super Intelligent

There are people who are super intelligent.

They can accomplish just about anything that they put their minds to.

Super intelligent people are usually rich people who get things done.

There are super intelligent people in every race, creed and color of people.

There are many super intelligent people who don't believe in Jesus Christ.

Jesus had perfect intelligence when He lived here on earth.

No one could ever outsmart Jesus in what they say and what they do.

Super-intelligence is from God, who gives super-intelligence to whoever He wants to give it to.

Many super intelligent people are full of pride.

They boast about themselves because they believe they are so great.

Many super intelligent people don't believe that there is a God who is so much more intelligent than them.

Where were the super intelligent people when God created the heavens and the earth?

Where were the super intelligent people when God created the sun, moon and all the stars?

Where were the super intelligent people when God created nature?

Where were the super intelligent people before the flood?

They didn't believe Noah when he told them that it would rain for forty days and forty nights.

Obedience to God is greater than super-intelligence, which will always fall short of the glory of God.

But I Love

Life is not easy, but I love believing in You, my Lord Jesus Christ.

Life is not easy, but I love worshiping You, my Lord.

Life is not easy, but I love obeying You, my Lord.

Life is not easy, but I love trusting You, my Lord.

Life is not easy, but I love writing poems about You, my Lord.

Life is not easy, but I love having my poems produced into songs about You, my Lord.

Life is not easy, but I love praying to You, my Lord.

Life is not easy, but I love depending on You, my Lord.

Life is not easy but I love being a witness of You, my Lord..

Life is not easy but I love living my life to do Your holy will, my Lord.

Life is not easy but I love being humble unto You, my Lord.

Up to This Day

Ever since we've been alive, only the Lord knows everything that we've seen up to this day.

Ever since we've been alive, only the Lord knows every word that we said up to this day.

Ever since we've been alive, only the Lord knows what we've done up to this day.

Ever since we've been alive, only the Lord knows our every move up to this day.

Ever since we been alive, only the Lord knows our every intention up to this day.

Ever since we been alive, only the Lord knows everywhere we've been up to this day.

Ever since we've been alive, only the Lord knows our every thought up to this day.

Ever since we been alive, only the Lord knows everything that we've felt up to this day.

Ever since we been alive, only the Lord knows every mistake that we've made up to this day.

Ever since we've been alive, only the Lord knows every good thing that we've done up to this day.

Ever since we been alive, only the Lord knows every wrong thing that we've done up to this day.

Ever since we been alive, only the Lord knows all of our good days.

Ever since we've been alive, only the Lord knows all of our bad days.

There is nothing that the Lord doesn't know up to this day and forever more days to come when the Lord Jesus Christ comes back again.

Look in the Mirror of Self

Look in the mirror of self to see what spiritual gifts that the Lord has given you to uplift your brothers and sisters in Jesus Christ the Lord.

Look in the mirror of self to see if you have the gift to preach God's holy word to anyone who will hear, even on the streets.

Look in the mirror of self to see if you have the gift to teach God's holy word to anyone who will hear you and want to reach out to tell others about what they learned.

Look in the mirror of self to see if you have the gift to write inspirational poetry for others to read so they can see some light shining in their path that Jesus wants to shine in.

Look in the mirror of self to see if you have the gift to heal someone's broken heart so they can feel the love of Jesus so very real.

Look in the mirror of self to see if you have the gift of love to show to everyone that you love them like Jesus loves them above their sins that He can save them from.

Look in the mirror of self to see if you have the gift to give Jesus your time to spend with Him in prayer, Bible study and working for Him to win souls to Him to be saved.

In the Bag of Life

You and I will go to the grocery store and buy some food to eat.

The checkout clerk will put your food in a plastic bag after its paid for.

We need some bags to carry our food in.

The Lord created this world and the sun, moon and stars and put it in the bag of life.

The Lord created the animals and a man and woman and put them in the bag of life.

Only the Lord can fill up the bag of life with his blessings.

Only the Lord can pick up the bag of life and carry it in His almighty hand.

The Lord will carry our dreams in the bag of life.

The Lord will put all good things in the bag of life and give it to us so we can take out those good things to use day after day.

The Lord will put wisdom and knowledge in the bag of life.

The Lord will put healing and deliverance in the bag of life.

The Lord will put love and truth in the bag of life.

The Lord will put all that we need in the bag of life.

The devil can't steal what the Lord put in the bag of life.

You and I can't empty the bag of life, no matter what good things we take out of it.

Many People Realize

Many people realize that life, health and strength are more valuable than anything else in this world.

During this coronavirus pandemic, many people truly care about their life, health and strength and they don't want to lose these things.

Many people want to live through this pandemic.

So many people realize that without life, health and strength they can't do anything.

If we are sick, we are weak and can't do much of anything for ourselves.

This coronavirus pandemic helps us all to realize that our life, health and strength are more valuable than anything else in this world.

If we are on our sick-bed, we will know that our life, health and strength is a treasure to us.

If we are on our sick-bed, we will know that we are missing out on health and strength.

If we are on our sick-bed, we will realize that life, health and strength is from the Lord.

This coronavirus pandemic has caused so many people to realize that their life, health and strength is more worth having than anything else in this world.

Unbelievers Will Not Be Attracted to Our Faith

Unbelievers will not be attracted to our faith in Jesus if they see that we are talking like them.

Unbelievers will not be attracted to our faith in Jesus if they see that we are dressing like them.

Unbelievers will not be attracted to our faith in Jesus if they see that we are doing the things that they do.

If unbelievers see that we are telling lies like them, they will not be attracted to our faith in Jesus.

If unbelievers see that we are living in adultery, they will not be attracted to our faith in Jesus.

If unbelievers see that we are fornicating like them, they will not be attracted to our faith in Jesus.

If unbelievers see that we are like them, they will not be attracted to our faith in Jesus.

If we are like an unbeliever, how can we have faith in Jesus?

They won't be attracted to our faith in Jesus because they won't see our faith in Jesus.

We can't have faith in Jesus and live our lives like unbelievers.

We can't fool the unbelievers who can see that we are supposed to be different from them.

We will only fool ourselves if we believe that we have faith in Jesus Christ while at the same time we have no change in our lives that makes us no different from unbelievers.

We Can say and Do

We can say good words and some people will criticize what we say.

We can do good deeds and some people will criticize what we do.

No matter what good words we say, some people won't like what we say.

No matter what good deeds we do, some people won't like what we do.

Some church folks will criticize the good deeds we do.

They claim to say good words about the Lord.

They claim to do good deeds for the Lord, but they are not pleased with you and me who are saying good words about the Lord and doing good deeds for the Lord.

Some church folks will get jealous of you and me and will criticize us for saying good words and doing good deeds.

They are not blessed by our ministry work for the Lord because they believe that we are not good enough to be on their spiritual level.

You and I can say good words, and some people just won't care to listen and wise up.

You and I can do good deeds, and some people just won't believe that the good we do is true.

We can love and obey our Lord and Savior Jesus Christ and some church folks will falsely accuse us of playing church in their eyesight of judgement.

Mental Health and Physical Health

If we are in good mental health and in good physical health, we have a chance to prosper in life.

There are people who are in good mental health and in good physical health, when they are lazy.

Who can prosper in life by not wanting to do anything?

If we are in good mental health and good physical health, we have a chance to live a good life.

If we have good mental health but our physical health is not so good, we can still prosper in some ways.

If we lose our mental health, there is no way that we can achieve anything in life.

If we lose our physical health, we still have a mind to help someone else do what is right.

Even the poorest person can do better if he or she has good mental health and good physical health.

It's very hard for someone to prosper in life if our mental health and physical health is not good.

If we lose our mind, we have no chance to get anywhere in life.

If we lose our physical health and still have our mental health, we have a chance to be a blessing to someone else.

Good mental health and good physical health is a gift from the Lord who doesn't cause anyone's health to go bad.

You and I can cause our own health to go bad, especially if we're disobeying the Lord.

The Government

The government has so much bad stuff going on every day.

Many of our nation's leaders are so deceptive and so greedy for worldly power and gain.

If it's not one thing then it's another bad thing going on in the political arena.

The government has so many crooked leaders who are so selfish and only look out for themselves.

Many of our government leaders will say one thing and do another thing.

Many of them will not do what they say for the citizens of our nation.

Many of them have failed we people of this nation.

Many government leaders just can't be trusted day after day.

Many of them are only talk — they make great speeches and don't follow through with what they say.

One day soon, Jesus Christ will come back again and set up His government of righteousness.

Jesus will create a new heaven and a new earth for all of His righteous children.

You and I will live forever under Jesus' government paradise if we are saved in Him.

My Mother's Prayers

My mother's prayers unto the Lord have a lot to do with me being here today, that I don't want to willfully sin against my Lord and Savior Jesus Christ.

My mother's prayers unto the Lord have a lot to do with me doing as well as I am today when I've been through some terrible times that could have killed me.

My mother's prayers have a lot to do with me confessing and repenting of my sins and giving my life unto the Lord Jesus Christ who loves me more than I can ever imagine.

My mother prayed for me, but I just didn't know how hard she prayed because I was so spiritually blind and could not see that Jesus died for my sins.

My mother prayed for me to be saved in Jesus before my life ends.

My mother is no longer in the land of the living, but I believe that I will see her again when Jesus Christ comes back again to receive her and me on the clouds of glory as we go back to heaven with Him along with all who are saved in him.

Is known

The air is known for us to breathe in and out of our nostrils.

The sun is known to give us its light all day long.

The moon is known to give us its glow all night long.

The stars are known to give us their sparkles all night long.

Sermons are known to give us faith in the Lord.

Books are known to be read.

Life is known for us to live.

Eyes are known for us to see.

Ears are known for us to hear.

Hands are known for us to hold something.

Food is known for us to eat.

Water is known for us to drink.

Love is known for us to treat one another right.

Death is known in the graveyards.

Jesus Christ is known in the Bible.

Jesus Christ is known in our belief in Him.

Jesus Christ is known in our renewed life.

We Love Life

We love life that we enjoy to live day after day, and no one in their right mind would want to die.

We love life that we love for our pets to live day after day, and it's the Lord who loves to give us life.

Anyone who loves life is in good mental health and only evil people would want to take the breath out of someone's life.

Only someone who's very depressed would want to take their own life.

We people who are in our right minds love life to the fullest and we love to live.

We Christians especially love life that we would give up for Jesus Christ's holy namesake if we truly love Him.

We love life even if we have to take someone else's life in self-defense.

Soldiers in war and police officers know this too well.

They love life, but they know that they have to take life away from those who could take their life away from them.

It's Helping Me

If my spiritual gifts are not helping anyone else to hold onto the Lord, they're helping me to hold onto the Lord.

If my ministry work is not helping anyone else to hold onto the Lord, it's helping me to hold onto the Lord.

I know that everybody will not be blessed by the poems that I write about my Lord and Savior Jesus Christ.

I know that everybody will not be blessed by my poems being produced into songs about my Lord and Savior Jesus Christ.

The most important thing to me is that what I do in Jesus' name is helping me to keep my faith and hope and trust in my Lord and Savior Jesus Christ.

I know that my works are not in vain because my works are helping me to deny myself and pick up my cross and follow Jesus Christ every day.

If my poems and songs about the Lord are not helping me to love and obey the Lord, then why should I want them to help others to love and obey the Lord?

I know that my works for the Lord can't save me from my sins, but my works can surely help me to believe in Jesus Christ every day.

You Are So Realistic All the Time

Oh Lord, You are so realistic all the time, Your love is so realistic and so divine.

Oh Lord, You can show us things that have real meaning.

O Lord, You can show us things that have real value.

Oh Lord, You are so realistic every day that You are very real in Your holy word that says if we love You we will keep Your commandments.

Oh Lord, You can show us people real feelings.

Oh Lord, You can show us real loving people.

Oh Lord, You are so realistic in your love that is for all men, women, boys and girls to make it to heaven above.

Oh Lord, You can show us what is real in this life.

O Lord, You can show us what is real in our hearts.

Oh Lord, You are so realistic in whatever You say and do in our lives that only You can bless so real through the thick and thin of life.

The Early Morning Light

When we see the early morning light, God's mercy is made new upon us in the angel's eyesight.

When we see the early morning light, God's grace will favor us to make things right with God.

When we see the early morning light, God's love is upon our lives for us to see another day of thanking God for life.

When we see the early morning light, God's will is for us to live by what God made so real.

When we see the early morning light, the price that Jesus Christ paid for us shines so bright like the sunlight.

When we see the early morning light, God's Son, Jesus Christ, is representing our case in the highest heights in heaven in the early morning light of God's almighty love.

Some Things Do Come Up

Some things do come up and will get in the way of our plans for the day.

We can get discouraged when things come up and get in our way, and this can cause our cup of joy to turn over and spill out our peace of mind.

We just don't like it when something comes up so unexpectedly that we just don't know about.

We can have our hopes up high when something comes up and tries to make us feel down.

When this happens, we need to keep our eyes on Jesus Christ who can give us the strength to get through the things that can come up under the great blue sky.

No matter what things come up, you and I can always pray to Jesus to work things out for us. When this happens, we must pray to Jesus to remove the bad things that can come up in our lives.

Life is Always Up to Something

Life can show us how good people can be.

Life can show us how bad people can be.

Life is always up to something.

Life can show us how bad the weather can get.

Life can tell us many good, real, true stories.

Life is always up to something.

Life can tell us many bad stories.

Life can show us the truth about ourselves.

Life is always up to something.

Life can show us lies about ourselves.

Life can reveal to us that Jesus is the source of the life.

Life is always up to something.

Life can take us through some changes.

Life can cause us to appreciate our lives, especially when death knocks on our door.

Life is always up to something and Jesus Christ always knows about it.

There are a Lot of Good People

There are a lot of good people in this world who are not Christians.

They will treat you and me better than many Christians do.

They will talk to you and me better than many Christians do.

Many people don't care if you and I are a Christian or not a Christian.

They really care about you and me treating them right.

There are a lot of good people in this world who have wrong beliefs.

They don't let this stop them from treating people right.

We Christians have the right belief.

We believe in Jesus Christ, but we don't do people any good if we treat them bad.

The Lord knows everybody's heart, and He surely knows how to convict people to feel guilty about treating people bad.

All good things come from the Lord whose goodness can lead people to repent of their sins.

No matter what age we are, we all belong to the Lord whose time is not our time.

On our time we can want to try to change people to believe in Jesus Christ to do His will.

There are a lot of good people who are not Christians, but they will love you and me more than a lot of so-called Christians do.

No Matter What We Do for the Lord

No matter what we do for the Lord, some people will not be blessed by what we do for the Lord.

Some people in the church will not like all of your sermons.

Some people in the church will not like all of your songs.

Some people in the church will not like all of your inspired poems.

Some people in the church will not like all of your Sabbath school teachings.

No matter what we do for the Lord, we need to always improve on what we do for the Lord.

The Lord will help us to improve in our ministries, as long as we have the right motives to improve.

The Lord truly knows that some church folks won't be blessed by what we do in His holy name.

Those church folks believe that their ministry work is better than your ministry work and my ministry work.

They don't know what it truly means to pray for you and me to improve in our ministry work for the Lord.

No matter what we do for the Lord, some church folks believe that they are so much more gifted than us.

We Can Tell Jesus

We can tell Jesus about our fears — Jesus doesn't mind taking the time out to hear about them.

We can tell Jesus about our grief, because Jesus will never leave us like our deceased loved ones did.

We can tell Jesus about our weakness, and He will strengthen us so we know that we can give Him all our trust.

We can tell Jesus about our heartaches so that He can relieve us of our sadness and help us to move on and see how much He loves us.

We can tell Jesus about anything that we feel, because He understands us completely and so real.

He knows us better than we will ever understand ourselves in this world where sin has polluted all the land.

Jesus tells us about His victory over every sin that the devil tempted Him with when he lived in this world before sinful men.

Is Eternal

Praising You, my Lord Jesus, is eternal.

Worshipping You, my Lord Jesus, is eternal.

Needing You, my Lord Jesus, is eternal.

Believing in You, my Lord Jesus, is eternal.

Trusting You, my Lord Jesus, is eternal.

Hope in You, my Lord Jesus, is eternal.

Following You, my Lord Jesus, is eternal.

Obeying You, my Lord Jesus, is eternal.

Depending on You, my Lord Jesus, is eternal.

Holding on to You, my Lord Jesus, is eternal.

Loving You, my Lord Jesus, is eternal.

Victory in You, my Lord Jesus, is eternal.

Truth in You, my Lord Jesus, is eternal.

Life eternal is in You, my Lord Jesus Christ, who created all things in heaven and on earth.

Under the Sky

Under the sky we will go through some changes in this life.

Under the sky we will have some good days and some bad days.

Under the sky we will have some disappointments.

Under the sky people can fail us.

Under the sky people can lie to us.

Under the sky people can break the laws.

Under the sky people can get full of pride.

Under the sky we need God's mercy and grace.

Under the sky Jesus Christ lived on earth without sin.

Under the sky a few people are truly good Christians.

Under the sky we can shorten our own life.

Under the sky people can show partiality.

Under the sky people can get their hearts broken.

Under the sky people can believe in Jesus Christ and be saved.

Under the sky Christians can get filled with the Holy Ghost.

In the Mirror of Life

In the mirror of life, we have some fear of the unknown that may not be so far away but may be very near to us.

In the mirror of life, we have some moles of disappointment that we will see sooner or later.

In the mirror of life, we have some pimples of doubt and we don't know what can come in and leave out of our lives.

In the mirror of life, we have some wrinkles of grief that can't be overlooked in the morning, noon and in the evening hours as we grieve over a loved one who has passed away.

In the mirror of life, we have some dry skin tissues of sins needing to be confessed unto the Lord whose mirror of love will wipe away our teardrops.

In the mirror of life, we have some weight of burdens to bear after eating the food of selfishness that the Lord will never serve us.

One Day I Want to See Jesus Christ

One day, I want to see Jesus Christ who I believe in.

One day, I want to see Jesus Christ who I love.

One day, I want to see Jesus Christ who I put my hope in.

One day, I want to see Jesus Christ who I put my trust in.

One day, I want to see Jesus Christ who I have put my faith in.

One day, I want to see Jesus Christ who I obey.

One day, I want to see Jesus Christ who I live for.

One day, I want to see Jesus Christ who I want to be with.

One day, I want to see Jesus Christ who I will follow.

One day, I want to see Jesus Christ who I love to hold onto.

One day, I want to see Jesus Christ who I dream about seeing.

One day, I want to see Jesus Christ who is worthy to be praised.

One day, I want to see Jesus Christ who created all things.

One day, I want to see Jesus Christ who died on the cross for my sins.

One day, I want to see Jesus Christ who can save me from my sins.

One day, I want to see Jesus Christ who can cleanse me from my sins.

One day, I want to see Jesus Christ who is coming back again on the clouds of glory.

Won't Make Any Time for You

Many people won't make any time for you, oh Lord.

They will make time to do other things that they will put before You.

Many people will make time to travel here and there, but won't make time for You, my Lord who is everywhere no matter where we go.

God cares for and protects you and me.

Many people will make time to spend their money, but they won't make any time for you, oh Lord, who's always so divine to supply all of our needs through the day and through the night.

Many people will make time to work for men, but not for God.

Oh Lord, my God, You are the creator of all things that You can bring to an end.

Many people won't make any time to work for You, my Lord, who will never hurt anyone's heart for working for You who will never make anyone work overtime.

Many people won't make any time for You, my Lord Jesus Christ, who came from heaven and made time to give up Your life to save all sinners from being lost in our sins.

Some Things We Do Wrong

Some things we do wrong we can regret for a lifetime.

Some things we do wrong can last for a lifetime.

Some things we do wrong will surely catch up with us.

We can surely do some wrong things in our lives for not waiting on the Lord.

We can try to get ahead of the Lord and do things of our own will.

Doing things of our own will can surely cause us to do some wrongs that can last all of our lifelong days.

The Lord is merciful with us because He bears living with the wrongs we can do.

Some things we do wrong will be seen in our lives for a long time.

Some things we do wrong can surely affect others for a long time.

Some things we did wrong in the past years will let us know what a fool we were.

Some things we did wrong in the past years will surely let us know how ignorant we were.

Some things we do wrong will never let us forget our wrongs.

Jesus will forgive us all of our sins and cast them in the deepest sea.

Especially in the Church

We Christians are supposed to love one another, especially in the church.

We are not supposed to treat someone better than someone else.

We are supposed to treat everyone the same way, with love.

There is no little me and big you in the church.

There are church folks who will treat someone better than someone else.

The people of the world love to do that.

There are church folks who will love you if you are educated.

There are church folks who will love you if you have plenty of money.

There are Christians who believe that they are above you and me in righteousness.

There are Christians who will come to church and act like you and I are not good enough to be there in their eyesight.

We Christians are supposed to love everyone — educated or not educated.

We Christians are supposed to be like Jesus Christ, who loves everyone the same way.

Jesus Christ our Lord says, "You are not my disciples if you don't have love for one another."

The Lord Can Use Illnesses

The Lord can use illnesses to help us keep our faith in Him.

The Lord can use illnesses to help us keep our hope in Him.

The Lord can use illnesses to help us keep our trust in Him.

The Lord can use illnesses to help us keep our eyes on Him.

The Lord can use illnesses to help us pray to Him.

The Lord can use illnesses to help us depend on Him.

The Lord can use illnesses to help us to hold onto Him.

The Lord can use illnesses to help us to obey Him.

The Lord can use illnesses to help us to love Him.

The Lord can use illnesses to help us give to Him the glory and the praise.

We all know that being ill is not a good thing for our mind or body.

Only the Lord can make something good out of an illness.

The Lord can do anything but fail you and me.

The Lord can use illnesses to help us to confess and repent of our sins.

We Can Shape Our Own Lives

We can shape our own lives by the choices that we make.

God gives us all free will to shape our own lives.

Lucifer and the fallen angels shaped their own lives by their free will choices up in heaven.

They fell from heaven because of shaping their lives to sin against God.

Adam and Eve shaped their own lives and disobeyed God.

God will shape our lives if we love Him and keep His commandments day after day.

Many people will shape their lives to shorten their lives by making bad choices.

Many people have shaped their lives into an early grave by rebelling against God.

We can shape our own lives for doing our own will.

God will shape our lives for doing His holy will.

God had shaped his Son Jesus Christ's life because Jesus totally submitted His will and total obedience unto His heavenly Father when Jesus lived on earth without sin.

God can only shape our lives if we confess and repent and give our lives to Him.

The Only Way

The only way I can be happy is in You, my Lord.

The only way I can be content is in You, my Lord.

The only way I can be good is in You, my Lord.

The only way I can be right is in You, my Lord.

The only way I can be satisfied is in You, my Lord.

The only way I can live right is in You, my Lord.

The only way I can talk right is in You, my Lord.

All good things come from You, my Lord.

All right things come from You, my Lord.

The only way I can be complete is in You, my Lord.

The only way I can love everybody is in You, my Lord.

The only way I can be save is in You, my Lord.

The only way I can go to heaven is in You, my Lord Jesus Christ.

You Became a Man

Lord Jesus, You became a man to relate to men.

Lord Jesus, You became a man to save men from their sins.

Lord Jesus, You became a man for men to have no excuse to not be saved from their sins.

Lord Jesus, You became a man to live without sin among men.

Lord Jesus, You became a man to give men salvation in You.

Lord Jesus, You became a man to give men hope in You.

Lord Jesus, You became a man to give men the victory over their sins.

Lord Jesus, You became a man for every boy and girl to grow up being saved in You.

Lord Jesus, You were born without sin and became a man without sin to be the light of the world.

Lord Jesus, You became a man to let every man, woman, boy and girl know Your will by keeping Your commandments.

Right Now

Right now, so many people don't have any food to eat.

Right now, so many people don't have clean water to drink.

Right now, so many people don't have a roof over their heads.

Right now, so many people don't have clean clothes to wear.

Right now, so many people can't take a shower.

Right now, so many people are out of work.

Right now, so many people are sick.

Right now, so many people are dying.

Right now, so many people are being abused.

Right now, so many people are living in fear for their lives.

Right now, everybody needs Jesus Christ.

Right now, Jesus wants to save everybody.

Right now, so many people are lost in their sins.

Right now, we are saved in Jesus if we believe in Him.

Passing Through Time

We are passing through time that is short for all of us.

We can't put our trust in time that is passing through this world.

We are passing through time that is unpredictable.

We are passing through time that has no guarantee to always be here.

Time is not always on our side.

Many people believe they have plenty of time left to live.

Many people believe they have plenty of time left to accomplish things in this life.

Many people believe they have plenty time left to get their lives in order.

Many people believe they have plenty time left to deny self and pick up their crosses and follow Jesus Christ.

We are all passing through time that can't promise us we'll live to see another day.

We are passing through time like driving on a bridge and not knowing when we have to stop for the gates to open and let the ships pass through to get on the other side.

We are passing through time that is running out in this world for Jesus to come back again.

www.ingramcontent.com/pod-product-compliance
Lightning Source LLC
Chambersburg PA
CBHW070113080526
44586CB00013B/1283